IMAGES OF TRANSPORT

RAILWAY DISASTERS

IMAGES OF TRANSPORT

RAILWAY DISASTERS

Simon Fowler

PEN & SWORD
TRANSPORT

First published in Great Britain in 2013 and reprinted in 2021by
PEN & SWORD TRANSPORT
an imprint of
Pen & Sword Books Ltd
47 Church Street, Barnsley
South Yorkshire S70 2AS

ISBN 978-1-84563-158-1

Typeset by Mac Style, Bridlington, East Yorkshire
Printed and bound in Great Britain by CPI Group (UK) Ltd, Croydon,
CRO 4YY

Pen & Sword Books Ltd incorporates the imprints of Pen & Sword
Archaeology, Atlas, Aviation, Battleground, Discovery, Family
History, History, Maritime, Military, Naval, Politics, Railways, Select,
Social History, Transport, True Crime, Claymore Press, Frontline
Books, Leo Cooper, Praetorian Press, Remember When, Seaforth
Publishing and Wharncliffe.

For a complete list of Pen & Sword titles please contact:
Pen & Sword Books limited
47 Church Street, Barnsley, South Yorkshire, S70 2AS, England.
E-mail: enquiries@pen-and-sword.co.uk
Website: www.pen-and-sword.co.uk

Contents

Introduction   6

Chapter 1   Accidents on the Early Railway 1829–1889   39

Chapter 2   The Golden Age of the Railway Accident 1890–1914   57

Chapter 3   The Years of War and Peace 1914–1947   83

Chapter 4   Accidents on British Railways 1948–1968   99

Further Reading   122

Introduction

Railway crashes are now incredibly rare. This happy position is the work of nearly two hundred years learning from experience and a lot of trial and error. In this book we are going to look at some of the most famous accidents as well as many that have been forgotten about, even by the railway enthusiast.

Put simply the history of the railway accident is basically a history of shutting the engine shed after the train has come off the track, that is the study of the introduction of technologies and systems to prevent particular accidents happening again. Sometimes the answers are simple – ensuring signalmen and driver don't lose concentration as the result of working long shifts – and sometimes the answers are complicated – introducing technologies to prevent trains going through red signals.

Most accidents are of course minor events, soon forgotten even by the people they involved. In two typical months – January and February 2010 – for example, there were thirteen reported incidents. Three trains collided with cars on unmanned crossings or the doors of driver's cabs swung open due to poor maintenance, and two freight trains derailed. Nobody was killed, although two dozen people were injured, fortunately none seriously.

It would be wrong to think railway safety improvements were introduced without opposition. Inevitably they were expensive and it was argued that because the railways were always relatively safe they were largely unnecessary. Railway companies were also fearful of the loss of profits their introduction might mean coupled with a fervent belief that government should not interfere in their business. And managers, initially, also argued their introduction would lead to lazy staff. Sir Richard Moon, Chairman of the London & North Western Railway, argued in the 1870s: "These mechanical appliances were all inducements to inattention on the part of signalmen and drivers."

American railway operators mocked the British counterparts' indifference to safety. The London correspondent of the *New York Times* in the 1870s wrote: "If the choice lay between going safely and at moderate speed, or going fast with a good chance of being killed, most Englishmen would unhesitatingly pronounce for the latter."

The worst decade for safety was probably the 1870s. Investment in the permanent way and signalling had not kept up with the increasing number of trains travelling at ever-faster speeds. As a result accidents were inevitable. At Wigan on 3 August 1873, for example, thirteen people were killed and thirty injured when an express train from Euston to Scotland crashed into the station. The Railway Inspector concluded the crash was due to "excessive speed" and castigated the LNWR for permitting it.

Pressure for improvements came from two sources. Firstly there was public pressure to run as safe a railway as possible reflected in press stories about railway accidents. Newspapers, national and regional, ran endless stories about collisions, crashes and the resulting casualties.

The crash at Wigan in September 1873 was caused by speeding through the station. It resulted in thirteen deaths and thirty injuries. The terrible impact of the collision was captured here by the *Illustrated London News*. Credit SSPL 10411987

In the decade of the 1870s the *Manchester Guardian*, alone, ran at least one story in every issue about a railway disaster of one kind or another.

Britain's most influential newspaper *The Times* took up the cause, fulminating after the Wigan crash in September 1873: "It is a national scandal, after a collision or other accident that has numbered its victims by the score to have to proclaim that the whole was due to the want of a continuous brake, or a locked connecting rod, or of some other mechanical contrivance as well known and as effectual as the lock on a street door." And for a while it had a column headed "Friday's railway accidents" along the lines of "Court and Social".

Heavy-handed barbs against the railway companies and their complacency filled the pages of *Punch*, for example. The new St Pancras station opened in 1868, for example, was

PATENT FIRST-CLASS COSTUME FOR THE COLLISION SEASON

Traveller. "Yes, it's decidedly warm, but there's a feeling of security about it I rather like." (*Yawns.*) "Any chance of a smash to-day!?" [*Drops off to sleep!*

In the 1860s *Punch* advised its readers to dress for safety in the case of a railway smash. Credit Taylor Collection

nicknamed St Pancrash. And in *Punch's* 'Tourist's Alphabet' 'S' stood for 'the smash *THAT* is "nobody's fault".'

The press had a field day with the Armagh crash in June 1889 when eighty people, mainly children, were killed and another 260 injured as the result of railway incompetence. It was the worst accident yet on the railways. Stories, like this one from the *Manchester Guardian* for 15 June 1889, filled the pages:

> Today, like yesterday, is a day of funerals and tokens of grief and sorrow are met with at every point. A large number of interments took place yesterday evening, but the majority of the victims are being buried today. Hearses may be seen in almost every street. The engine of the train that collided remains in its original position upturned and embedded in the embankment. Numerous visitors have been to the scene of the accident today and many a camera has focused on the wrecked train. Carriage doors and windows lie mixed up with men's and girls' hats, women's bonnets, buns, bread, parasols, iron flanges, boots, portions of dresses and umbrellas. All these articles bear traces of the crash.

The accident caused huge public outrage. Queen Victoria telegraphed the town council from Balmoral: "The Queen is anxious to know how the injured are progressing." The government acted remarkably swiftly introducing legislation imposing minimum safety standards on railway companies. Most railways, however, already met the standards and those that did not were given four years to improve matters. Even so the accident was probably the most significant in British history. As Tom Rolt notes in *Red for Danger*.

> ... the Armagh disaster represents a most significant milestone in railway history, possibly, indeed, the most significant of all. For... the old happy-go-lucky days of railway working came to their ultimate end and the modern phase of working as we know it began.

One hundred and ten years later relentless media pressure exposed the short-comings of Railtrack after the Hatfield crash of 17 October 2000, forcing the government to in effect renationalise the company. Matters were not helped when the management, in the words of Matthew Engel, went into "headless chicken" mode for several months after the accident bringing the railway system almost to a halt. And *Private Eye* commented: "the trains are completely safe. There aren't any."

But quietly more influential was the Railway Inspectorate. Established in November 1840 as part of the Board of Trade, railway inspectors have investigated all but the most trivial accidents and made recommendations where appropriate to prevent similar accidents occurring in future. Their first investigation concerned the derailment of a train caused by the fall of a large casting from a wagon on a passenger train at Howden, in which four passengers were killed.

Inevitably the creation of the Inspectorate was opposed by the railways who resented interference in their business. The greatest of all railway engineers Isambard Kingdom Brunel told the committee that government inspectors would receive no cooperation from railwaymen who could scarcely be expected to assist in shackling themselves, although they would, *he hoped*, answer questions in a gentlemanly manner. Railway officials understood very well, he said, how to look after public safety and possessed more ability to find out what was necessary than any inspecting officer.

Inspectors could not insist on changes being introduced, all they could do was recommend they be made. As Tom Rolt suggested their motto should be "supervision without interference". The railway companies naturally were reluctant to spend more than they had to. In 1872, Richard Moon, the Chairman of the London and North Western Railway (second only to the Great Western in importance) grumbled to shareholders about an unfair division of responsibilities between railways and government, and that: "The Board of Trade insisted on signals and other works, that necessitated a large expenditure by the companies."

The Railway Inspectorate was recruited from retired Royal Engineer officers. They formed a small cadre of experts who built up considerable practical experience in all aspects of railway running. According to the American railway engineer and writer Charles Francis Adams in 1879, accidents were investigated by the same group of people who: "visit the spot and sifts the affair to the very bottom, locating responsibilities and pointing distinctly the measures necessary to guard against its repetition". However in the United States: "The same man never investigates two accidents, and for the one investigation he does make, he is competent only in his own esteem."

Railway Inspectors are still at work. These days, however, they are part of the Railway Accident Investigation Branch, an autonomous organisation reporting to the Department for Transport.

It is important to stress railways have always been a much safer form of travel for passengers than the alternatives. Charles Adams wrote in the 1870s: "A vague but deeply rooted conviction commonly prevails that the railroad has created a new danger: that because of it the average human being's hold on life is more precarious than it was." It is a perception that remains today judging by the hysteria in the press after the Hatfield crash in 2000 and comments made to the author at the time by friends and colleagues.

Yet the evidence is all to the contrary. Even in its infancy in the 1830s and 1840s, the railway was safer than the stagecoach, with its tendency to turn over at speed or throw off any passengers clinging to the roof. Charles Adams suggested accidents involving passengers were sixty times more likely than on the railways.

'The Pleasures of the Rail-Road' was a satirical coloured etching by Henry Hughes, published in 1831. It purported to illustrate the dramatic effects of a boiler exploding during a railway journey, although the artist had clearly never seen a train. Although there were a number of accidents of this kind the railway was always much safer than travelling by coach. Credit SSPL 10419914

However many railway travellers perceived nothing but danger in the new form of transport. As early as 1829, the politician Thomas Creevey described a journey as "really flying, and it is impossible to divest yourself of the notion of instant death to all upon the least accident happening".

To modern eyes railways, particularly those before the 1870s and 1880s when the first effective safety devices were introduced, were incredibly dangerous, yet few of the many guides published for passengers refer to the possibility of mishap. Perhaps this was because Victorian society was much more use to death and accidents.

One exception however was *The Railway's Traveller's Handy Book of Hints, Suggestions and Advice* published in 1862 with the most nervous of travellers in mind. For the utmost safety the anonymous author recommended "A seat in a first class carriage, opposite one which is unoccupied is safest, because the body is then opposed to the padded back of the carriage, and under these circumstances, seldom sustains serious injury." He advised his readers that in the case of a carriage overturning the passenger should attempt to "jump from the upper side as the carriages go over, and in taking this jump the feet should be placed together close together, the arms held close to the side, and the body inclined forward." And in the case of a collision, the writer suggested more sensibly "when a person has reason to anticipate a concussion, he should without hesitation throw himself onto the floor of the carriage".

There are surprisingly few eyewitness accounts of accidents. One of the most graphic was recorded by a reporter from the *Hampshire Telegraph*, who talked to a survivor of an accident at Peasmarsh on 9 September 1873, when the train ran into a bullock on the line. The unidentified lady appears to have been a first class passenger:

Suddenly the engine began whistling furiously and we heard the brakes strongly put down. My eldest brother hardly had time to exclaim 'what's up?' when there came an awful jolt which threw us all forward in a heap, then three or four more frightful jolts, and then a smashing crashing, clouds of dust, a shower of glass and splinters, and then a silence, broken by the nurse's exclamation, asking for the child. He was lying under me, with my arms one on each side of his head. In a minute we scrambled to our feet, asking each other if we were hurt and astonished to find that we were safe. We were saved as if by a miracle.

Our carriage was...completely turned on its side and one window was high above our heads, the other underneath.... The buffer and corner of the next carriage had come completely through into our compartment, and of course the whole side below us was completely smashed in. The cushions were very good and I think we owe our lives to that fact for if they had given way the splinters must have injured us. As it was the cushions were torn off and fell over and so protected us.... [eventually a ladder was lowered into the carriage and they clambered out].

Nearly the whole train lying on its side along the embankment, which itself was torn up a great deal, some of the carriages and unfortunately many of the people were almost buried in the earth. Some [of the carriages] appeared almost literally smashed to pieces. All round lay wounded and suffering people, many of whom appeared to be children.

The crash resulted in three deaths and unknown number of injuries.

Of course not everybody was killed in a railway accident. In many ways more serious were the physical and mental injuries caused by surviving a crash. Modern psychiatry recognises the traumas which a railway accident can cause, but our Victorian forebears were only beginning to investigate the phenomenon. An early study found that a railway accident had effects on the nervous system "quite beyond those of any ordinary injury" and a shock so severe it might "shatter the whole constitution" during a life that might "be expected to be curtailed in its duration" even though any external physical injuries might be slight.

These findings certainly fit the case of Charles Dickens who struggled to overcome the trauma caused by being involved in the crash at Staplehurst on 8 June 1865 (see page 42). Indeed it is likely the experience contributed to his death at the comparatively early age of 58 coincidentally on the fifth anniversary of the accident.

Dickens now found it difficult to travel by rail. A few days after the accident he wrote to a friend:

I cannot bear railway travelling yet. A perfect conviction, against the senses, that the carriage is down on one side (and generally that is the left, and not the side on which the carriage in the accident really went over) comes over me with anything like speed and is inexpressibly distressing.

A couple of years later two of his children watched their father on a train and noted: "as soon as it went across the points he would grab hold of his chair and look straight at the floor. He would sweat, he would tremble..."

A survivor of the Dunbar accident of 3 January 1898, C.E. Cockburn, Chief Superintendent of the Glasgow & South Western Railway, who had been one of the sleeping-car passengers told the Railway Inspector Lt Col HA Yorke at the subsequent enquiry: "I had suffered no inconvenience at the time, but 48 hours afterwards I suffered from nervous shock and subsequently had to take leave of absence." However, he doesn't seem to have been permanently traumatised by his experiences. For more about the accident see page 70.

Occasionally passengers enjoyed the experience. An anonymous correspondent to The Times wrote in November 1869, perhaps tongue in cheek, that previous to a trip to London from Manchester he had been suffering from rheumatic fever. On the journey south he had been involved in a crash:

From the moment of the collision to the present hour no ache, pain, sweat or tremor has troubled me in the slightest degree, and instead of being, as I expected and intended in bed, drinking *tinct. Aurantii*, or absorbing through my pores oil of horse chestnut, I am conscientiously bound to be at my office bodily sound.

He concluded by appealing to the paper not to print his name "or the Midland Company will come down on me for compensation."

In 1864 legislation was passed which allowed the victims of accidents to sue the railway companies. It was not always easy to differentiate between genuine victims and those who were making spurious claims. As a result the railway companies were often reluctant to pay up. In 1867, the South Eastern Railway tried to impose a limit of £100 on compensation payments, claiming "We have to pay large sums of money to people of a low class of life, and there is a desire on the part of solicitors and others to contrive at attempts to extort large sums of money from the railways."

It was possible to buy insurance against railway accidents. Most policies were sold by the Railway Passengers Assurance Company, which is now part of Aviva. Passengers could pay a supplement of three pence on a first-class ticket, two pence on a second-class ticket and a penny on a third-class ticket which, in the case of a fatal accident, would entitle their family to £1000, £500 and £200 respectively. In the cases where accidents were non-fatal, but there had been injury, the company would pay out "a sum of compensation that they consider just." Sales were made through booking offices and booking clerks received ten per cent of each policy sold.

In addition the purchase of a particular magazine or newspaper might entitle readers to claim compensation in case of accident. The first such scheme was started in 1885 by George Newnes, the proprietor of *Tit Bits,* who announced that "one hundred pounds will be paid by the proprietor of *Tit-Bits* to the next-of-kin of any person who is killed in a railway accident, provided a copy of the current issue of *Tit-Bits* is found upon the deceased at the time of the catastrophe." The first successful claimant was the family of a 40-year-old coachbuilder who had been killed after falling between the train and the platform at Hatfield station. The coroner proclaimed "accidental death". However, crucially, four witnesses testified that the man had *Tit-Bits* in his pocket. Other magazines followed suit. By 1892 relatives of readers of *Short Cuts* could claim £250 if their relation had been killed in a railway accident with a copy of the magazine in their pocket.

Railway safety has not been helped by passengers who disregard both the rules and basic common sense. In the early days many accidents were caused by the fact that neither the railway companies nor passengers had any experience of how they worked. They tended to assume that the 'Iron Horse', was literally no more than a metallic stage coach running in much the same way.

This reasoning lay behind the most famous railway death of all: the politician William Huskisson in 1830 at the opening of the Liverpool and Manchester Railway. He fell into the path of the oncoming *Rocket* engine while attempting to enter the Duke of Wellington's carriage. A horse might have shied away: the locomotive could not. The injured Huskisson,

The MP for Liverpool, William Huskisson, is famously the first man known to have been killed on the railways. The accident happened at the opening of the Liverpool and Manchester Railway on September 1830. Credit SSPL 10400297

whose leg was badly damaged, was rushed in a train driven by George Stephenson himself at the hitherto unknown speed of 30 miles per hour to a doctor in nearby Eccles. But it was to no avail he died shortly afterwards.

Huskisson's death was fairly unusual. A more common cause of accidents was foolish behaviour by passengers. One of the "Plain Rules" for railway travellers in Dr Dionysius Lardner's *Railway Economy*, published in 1850 warned passengers to "Beware of Yielding to the Sudden Impulse to Spring from the Carriage to Recover your Hat which has Blown off or a Parcel Dropped."

To prevent occurrences of this kind, carriages were often locked to prevent passengers entering or leaving during travel. This was not ideal. Many Victorians were worried about being locked in with murderers, madmen or almost as serious having to consort with complete strangers of an inferior social class. And such a practice was a serious hazard in case of an accident, when it was nearly impossible for passengers to escape. The practice began to be phased out after a crash on the newly opened line between Paris and Versailles in May

A painting of the 'Disaster on the Railway between Versailles and Bellevue, 8th May 1842' by Andre Provost. This was the first accident in which many passengers were killed. Estimates range between fifty-two and 200 but are known to include the explorer Jules Dumont d'Urville. The crash had a profound effect on railway development particularly in France. Credit Château de Sceaux, Musée de l'Ile-de-France

1842 where fifty-two passengers died, most burned to death in their locked carriages. Perhaps surprisingly, considering the inherent dangers lurking on the line, the Versailles crash was the first railway accident in which large numbers of passengers lost their lives.

Of course people continued to occasionally jump from fast moving trains – it was a fairly effective way to commit suicide after all. But a few passengers leapt for other reasons. The great cat burglar Charlie Peace was captured by police in London in January 1879 and returned to Sheffield a few days later where he was due to stand trial for murder. According to Charles Whibley in his 1910 *Book of Scoundrels*:

From the very commencement of the journey [Peace] had been wilful and troublesome. He kept making excuses for leaving the carriage whenever the train stopped. To obviate this nuisance the two warders, in whose charge he was, had provided themselves with little bags which Peace could use when he wished and then throw out of the window. Just after the train passed Worksop, Peace asked for one of the bags. When the window was lowered to allow the bag to be thrown away, Peace with lightning agility took a flying leap through it. One of the warders caught him by the left foot. Peace, hanging from the carriage, grasped the footboard with his hands and kept kicking the warder as hard as he could with his right foot. The other warder, unable to get to the window to help his colleague, was making vain efforts to stop the train by pulling the communication cord. For two miles the train ran on, Peace struggling desperately to escape. At last he succeeded in kicking off his left shoe, and dropped on to the line. The train ran on another mile until, with the assistance of some gentlemen in other carriages, the warders were able to get it pulled up. They immediately hurried back along the line, and there...they found their prisoner lying in the footway, apparently unconscious and bleeding from a severe wound in the scalp. A slow train from Sheffield stopped to pick up the injured man. As he was lifted into the guard's van, he asked them to cover him up as he was cold.

In addition there was always the possibility of people and animals being killed by passing trains as they tried to cross the tracks, unaware of oncoming locomotives. This was the cause of many railway accidents, which were rarely investigated by the Board of Trade, although coroner's juries would meet to consider circumstances and make recommendations for improvements if appropriate. One such accident occurred at Peasmarsh between Godalming and Guildford on 9 September 1873. Three people were killed when a Portsmouth to London train collided with a bullock that had escaped from a herd which was being moved to market in Guildford. The animal had crashed through a gate onto the line in front of the oncoming train. Remarkably the engine remained upright and unaffected by the collision, but the shock forced a number of the carriages down an embankment. Mrs Bridger of Old Godalming and her infant son, who were just travelling two stops to Guildford were among the casualties. Bizarrely the man she was sitting next to was uninjured.

Or people wandered on to the line without realising what they had done. This is what happened to the Russian anarchist Sergius Stepniak who lived in exile in the West London suburb of Bedford Park. On 23 December 1893 he set out to walk to Hammersmith for a meeting, when he was hit by a train of the North & South Western Junction Railway while crossing the line and killed. The coroner heard how the driver had blown his whistle and the stoker had shouted to no avail. One explanation is that, while a political prisoner in Turkey, he developed the power to shut out exterior sounds when he was thinking – "How else could I endure English dinner parties", he used to say. The writer Jerome K. Jerome, who had walked to Bedford Park with him from the Uxbridge Road on the previous Sunday, recalled that Stepniak was deep in talk and did not notice an approaching train on the crossing till Jerome plucked him by the sleeve out of harm's way.

More tragic were the number of suicides. From the earliest days men and women who wished to do away with themselves were attracted to the railways where it was easy to jump in front of fast moving trains with an almost inevitable result. One of the first involved an innkeeper at Redhill named Jupp who threw himself under the Brighton express. The *Reading Mercury* for 22 January 1842 reported he had been smashed to atoms. Less successful was an unnamed labourer from Wiltshire who was imprisoned in October 1841 for twice having tried to jump in front of oncoming trains.

Suicides on the railways are now by far and away the largest cause of death on the tracks and are next to impossible to prevent. The numbers remain relatively static. There are roughly 225 successful suicides or deaths thought to be suicides each year.

Signalling is key to the safe running of the railways. Its vital to know where each train is and to keep them at a safe distance from each other.

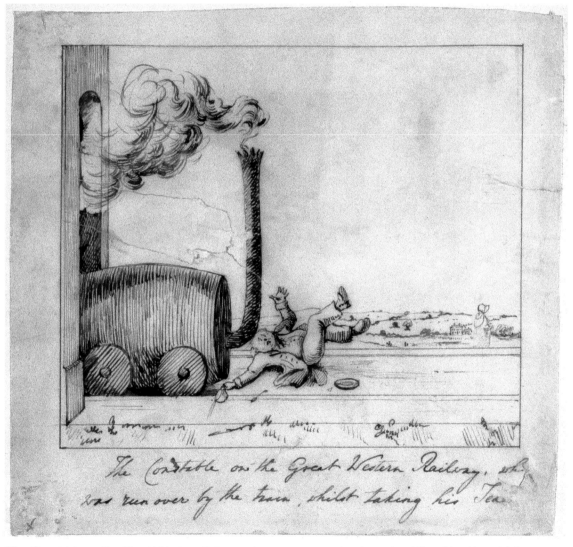

'The Constable on the Great Western Railway who was run over by the train whilst taking his tea'. Ink cartoon by Charles Alexander Saunders who was the first secretary of the Great Western Railway between 1833 and 1863. The cartoon reflects the cavalier attitude that all railway companies had to their staff. Railway policemen were familiar sights on the early permanent way as they acted as signalmen warning drivers of other trains ahead.
Credit SSPL 10328491

Originally signalling was by what is called the Time Interval System, that is trains were despatched at certain intervals after each other, much as stagecoaches had once been sent out from coaching inns. Policemen were positioned at key points along the line to give a 'stop' signal if a train had passed within ten minutes; a 'caution' if a train had passed between ten and seventeen minutes or otherwise a signal to proceed. It's not dissimilar to bus inspectors telling busses to wait in order to prevent bunching.

The time interval system could just about cope on a network when there was a fairly infrequent service. In the early days there might just be three or four trains a day even on mainlines. But

An engraving of a railway policeman acting as a signalman on the London & Brighton Railway. It was his job to ensure that trains did not pass into his section before they were due and to investigate if they were delayed. Credit SSPL 10453034

as more trains were laid on and speed increased it was becoming increasingly clear that it was no longer suitable.

The major flaw with this system was that there was no effective way of controlling trains if a preceding train was delayed for some reason. Train breakdowns, were very common in the early days. In such circumstances the policeman was supposed to run back a mile down the track to protect the train from oncoming traffic by showing a hand signal. At Lewisham, on 28 June 1857, eleven people were killed and many injured as two trains full of day-trippers collided with each other as a result in the breakdown in the time interval system.

The alternative was the Absolute Block System permitting only one train at a time to enter a section – or block – of track. Access was regulated by signals showing when it was safe to enter. At the beginning and end of each section there was a 'Home' signal indicating whether it was safe to enter the block or not. Once the train had passed into the block the Home signal would revert to danger.

Someway ahead of the Home signal was another warning signal – the 'Distant' signal. The approach of a home signal at danger was shown by the Distant signal warning the driver to slow down as the next signal would be at danger. Such signals would be placed sufficiently ahead of the Home signal to allow trains to stop in time if required.

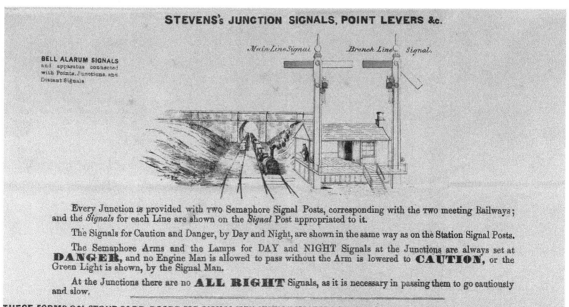

By the 1850s trains were increasingly regulated by the block system, whereby only one train was allowed in a particular block or space at times. Drivers knew whether it was safe to enter by the use of semaphore signals like those shown here. Men showing lights at night were soon replaced by oil lamps, much like modern traffic lights, fixed in the signals themselves. The most hated duty of signalmen was to clean and fill the lamps once a week. Credit TNA RAIL 189/18

The signal box and gantry array of signals outside Waterloo station in 1892. An increasingly complex signalling system ensured the safety of trains and their passengers. Credit TNA COPY 1/409

The signals themselves were positioned high up, with arms indicating whether a train could pass or had to halt. If the signal arm on one of these semaphore signals was set at horizontal – or danger – the block was occupied and no train could enter until the signal had changed. If the arm was at a sloping or upward angle of 45° then the section ahead was clear. The signals could be seen at night as they were lit by oil lamps. In busy areas lamp boys were employed to keep the oil lamps supplied, but in rural areas they were replenished by signalmen who loathed the work that was dirty and difficult, but of course absolutely necessary.

The signals were operated by signal boxes. Originally they would have been physically operated by railway staff, but increasingly they were operated using a system of levers and wires. Signal box would communicate with each other by telegraph, each box 'offering' the train to the next box as it progressed on its journey.

Inside a busy signal box on the Southern Railway in the 1920s. The levers moved points which directed the path taken by trains. It was a very responsible job – the slightest lapse in concentration could lead to disaster. Signal boxes have all but disappeared from the rail system replaced by centralised control centres. Credit TNA RAIL 1027/2 no24

With the exception of a few branch lines and on preserved railways, signals are now all electric, looking much like traffic lights, with red for 'do not proceed', amber for 'prepare to slow down' and green to proceed. Although they are much superior to semaphore signals occasionally drivers can fail to see them particularly when the sun is low in the sky. Badly positioned lights on the approaches to Paddington station lay behind the Ladbroke Grove accident in 1999.

In theory this was a simple and fool-proof system, but inevitably signalmen under stress forgot there were other trains on the line, as at Norton Fitzwarren in 1890 and Quintinshill in 1915. Various systems were introduced to try to prevent such occurrences.

To an extent, such accidents were prevented by introducing interlocking points and signals preventing any possibility of a train entering a section by mistake. From the 1860s on, the points

MUDDLEBY JUNCTION

Overworked Pointsman (puzzled). " Let's see !—there's the ' scursion ' were due at 4.45, and it ain't in ; then, afore that, were the ' mineral,'—no ! that must ha' been the ' goods,'—or the ' cattle.' No ! that were after,— cattle's shunting now. Let's see ! — fast train came through at—— Con-found ! — and here comes ' the express ' afore its time, and blest if I know which line she's on ! ! "

A *Punch* cartoon on the ease with which it was possible to confuse signal staff. As the drawing alludes, one very real danger was the running of special trains, such as boat trains to and from the Channel ports, outside the ordinary timetable, which meant that staff had to be extra alert. Credit Taylor Collection

and signals were grouped together in a single frame and were interlocked by mechanical bars and locking bolts. This ensured that if the points were set for a particular line only the signal levers for a particular line could be pulled to give clearance to a train. They were operated by levers.

As a further reminder many railway companies provided conspicuous red collars which were slipped over the levels in the signal box to show that a block has a stationary train in it (perhaps one loading or unloading coal). They both remind the signalman of the blockage and prevent the level being pulled by accident.

The signalman had one further duty. As each train passed out of his section he had to satisfy himself that it had not broken in two by checking the red lamp or disc positioned at the very end of the train. It was increasingly unusual for passenger trains to become uncoupled, but it was not unknown for this to occur on freight trains where there was no automatic braking system, so the driver might well be unaware his train had divided. If a train passed with a tail lamp unlit when it should be burning the signaller would inform the next signal box. If the train had become uncoupled he would attempt to attract the drivers attention to stop the train.

But what happens when the driver ignores the signal? It is easy enough to miss a signal at night, in bad weather or perhaps because the footplate crew had fallen asleep. Many accidents have occurred as a result. At Grantham on 14 September 1906, for example, fourteen people were killed and many injured when, for some unexplained reason, the driver ignored the Distant and Home signals set at danger near the station (see page 77). Why he did so remains a mystery.

Much thought was given to warning the driver of approaching signals and to stop the train if he ran through them. There have been a number of Automated Warning Systems (AWS), sometimes referred to as Automatic Train Control (ATC) or Automatic Train Protection (ATP). Modern trains are fitted with such systems, but it took many years for this to be the case. It has been estimated that between 1912 and 1957 a third of crashes, including the most serious ones of all at Quintinshill and Harrow and Wealdstone, could have been prevented had AWS been in operation. Even as late as 1997 Railtrack and the newly privatised railway companies were castigated about the lack of such systems after the Southall rail crash.

The first company to introduce AWS was the Great Western in 1906. As Adrian Vaughan observes, it "was an aid, a great reassurance in fog, and if the driver failed, a very effective last line of defence." It was fairly simple, but none the less effective. A fixed ramp between the rails made contact with a spring-loaded shoe on the locomotive. When the Distant signal was 'clear' an electric current passed through the ramp and rang a bell on the footplate. When the Distant signal was at 'caution' no current passed and the raising of the shoe broke an electrical circuit and sounded an alarm to warn the driver. It could also stop a train running at 70mph at the first stop signal after the ramp without being steam shut off. As a result, between 1906 and nationalisation in 1947 there was only one major accident on the GWR, at Norton Fitzwarren in 1940. It was not related to the Automatic Warning System.

On sections of railways where there was only one line, such as branch lines, most companies used a token or tablet system. At its simplest the driver wanting to enter the single-track section was given a token which he surrendered at the end of the section. Only trains carrying the token were allowed into the section. A more sophisticated development is the electric train token system, where each single-line section was provided with a pair of token instruments kept in the signal boxes at each end of the section. A token could be removed from one instrument only if both signalmen co-operated in agreeing to the release. Once a token has been removed, another cannot be removed until the token that is "out" is replaced in either instrument. Tokens from adjacent sections have different configurations to prevent them being inserted into the wrong instrument.

Signalmen communicated with each other and monitor the progress of trains on the blocks they were responsible for by telegraph. This allowed for messages to be sent almost instantly.

The weather could present problems, particularly fog, which could come down suddenly and obscure the signals. This is thought to be one of the reasons behind the Harrow and Wealdstone crash of 1952. The Raven Fog Signalling System installed on the London and North Eastern Railway between the wars was an attempt to alert drivers by ringing a bell on the foot plate when a signal was approaching. Credit RAIL 527/1239 (1)

Initially it was regarded as being little more than a novelty. In 1837 the London and Birmingham Railway built an experimental system between Euston and Camden Road. This worked well but the company decided not to put wires along the rest of their lines. A few years later the Great Western installed a system between Paddington and Slough. In 1844 news that Queen Victoria had given birth to a son was published on the streets of London within forty minutes of the message having being transmitted from Windsor Castle to Paddington along the wires.

These illustrations show a train delivering and receiving at a speed of fully 40 miles an hour.

We have found firemen able to do this with confidence without previous instruction and with only one or two trials at a slower speed.

On branch lines where there were few trains it was uneconomic to use the full block system. Instead at the beginning of the journey the train crew picked up a token which they surrendered at the end of the section. As there was only one token it meant that there was only one train on the line at a time. It worked well (and is still in use on some branch lines and heritage railways), but inevitably where there was confusion or the system circumvented, as at Abermule in 1921, disaster could result. Credit TNA MT 6/1847 (1)

The railway companies were slow to introduce the new technology. By 1870s only half the signal boxes were so connected.

The passage of a train was communicated between signal boxes by telegraph. Bells would ring indicating various messages. Two bells meant a train was entering section, while 1-3-1 asked if the line was clear for a parcels train, while 2-3-3 said a train was approaching in the wrong direction. The signalman receiving the signal was expected to confirm that he had received the message by repeating it back.

In large boxes there would have been a signal boy whose job was to record messages received in a register. In smaller boxes the register was completed by the signalman on duty. The register could be very useful in case of an accident, when it could provide clues about the events leading up to an accident. At Linlithgow on 4 October 1894, when a goods train became separated, the signalman Charles Milne produced his register. Just before the accident occurred he had received the following messages relating to the train:

offered from Loch Mill accepted at once 4.15am
'entered section' received 4.18am
'passed and entering section' given to Philpstoun 4.22am
offered to Philpstoun 4.24am
'Train out of section' received from Philpstoun 4.27am
All the block signals were properly given and received according to the rules.

At busy times it must sometimes have been a chore completing the register. And as a result could be neglected by the indolent. At Quintinshill in July 1915 it was left to James Tinsley, the man replacing George Meakin in the signal box to complete Meakin's entries, which had been scribbled on a scrap of paper. It was part of a private arrangement between the two signalmen allowing Tinsley to come on duty at 6.30am rather than at 6am – the correct time for change of shift. In doing so, he was not only breaking regulations he was also ignoring the chain of events leading up to Britain's worst ever rail disaster.

Another cause of many crashes were badly designed locomotives and carriages or the effects of accidents made much worse because of their flimsy construction.

Although undoubtedly beautiful in motion and on the platform it is safe to say that the steam locomotive was not really designed with safety in mind. Early engines were little more than boilers and gears on wheels with little consideration given either to the comfort of the men on the footplate or to the carriages they were hauling.

Particularly in the early years, when the principles of metallurgy were only hazily understood, they were inherently dangerous. Boilers in particular were liable to explode. On 1 April 1861 for example, the boiler of a Monmouthshire Railway goods engine exploded at the station. The Inspector reported:

> ... Two firemen were standing talking to each other on the foot plate of the engine when the boiler exploded; one was scalded in the back, and the other who belonged to the engine, was knocked off the footplate by the other fireman pushing against him, and fell on the ground, and had the bridge of his nose broken, and his shoulder and back contused. The driver, who was standing about 40 yards from the engine, was not hurt.

Such explosions could have their gruesomely humorous side. In *Engine Driving Life or Stirring Adventures and Incidents in the Lives of Locomotive Engine Drivers*, published in 1881, Michael Reynolds describes the fate of a Driver Legge, who was blown up with his boiler: "His arms and legs were hurled in different directions, and one of the former actually went through the window of a private house and fell upon a breakfast table round which the family were sitting at the time."

To take a minor example it was only with the arrival of diesel engines in the 1950s that locomotives began to be fitted with speedometers. Before then footplate crew gauged their speed from observing the passing of mileposts and listening to the clicks and clacks as the train went over the rails. The writer and signalman Adrian Vaughan was full of praise for "the steel nerve" of engine drivers "as they went into a wall of fog at 80mph with a passenger train" surviving:

> by their uncanny knowledge of the road, driving by feel of bumps and lurches, by the sequence of sounds from overbridges or underbridges, as well as keeping a check and tally on each station or signal box as they passed.... To drive your way through that lot,

Locomotives, especially the sleek express classes, were not always designed with the driver's visibility in mind. Except on the Great Western it was traditional for drivers to position themselves on the offside of the footplate which meant at crucial times he might not always see the signals. In situations like this he had to rely on the keen eyes of the fireman, who of course had his own duties. Here Driver F.A. Wilkes peers out and an unnamed fireman keeps the boilers stoked on the footplate of a British Railways Western Region express passenger steam locomotive in 1957. Credit SSPL 10452170

virtually blindfold, was a virtual performance rarely appreciated by anyone not of the footplate fraternity.

In addition, it was easy for a driver to miss signals if he was positioned on the wrong side of the engine. He might have to rely on his fireman. The fact the driver did not see signals at red outside Lewisham station was one of the causes of the Lewisham accident of 4 December 1957 where ninety lives were lost. However Driver Trew admitted in the subsequently enquiry that because he had never known the lights to be against him at this point he had not slowed down. It was not until his fireman shouted: "You have got a red" he hurriedly began to apply the emergency brake.

Because trains travelled so slowly in the early days braking was not considered terribly important. Trains were slowed down or brought to a halt by fairly primitive brakes operated by a guard on each carriage or on enough carriages to be effective. But as trains became faster, longer and heavier these brakes were no longer suitable. In fact they were very dangerous.

Attempts were made to devise a brake that was 'continuous' – one applied effectively and smoothly to every vehicle in a train at once, not just in an emergency. And one which was 'failsafe', so if the braking system was disrupted in any way the brakes would go on automatically.

The first such brakes began to be introduced in the 1860s. But the leader in the technology was the American George Westinghouse. He came to Britain in 1871 to try to sell his new system, but many companies were suspicious of anything that had not been developed on these shores. His system was actuated by air pressure, which if broken turned the brakes on. But many British companies preferred the inferior vacuum-brake system, because it was cheap to install. But it had a fatal flaw the vacuum pipe was easy to puncture and once this occurred the brake was useless.

In July 1884 there was a serious crash at Penistone in which twenty-four people were killed. The Inspector Major Marindin, however, concluded that had continuous brakes been in operation only a fairly minor accident would have occurred. Three years later in September 1887, another crash at Hexthorpe near Doncaster was also caused by the brakes. Another twenty-five passengers lost their lives. The driver and fireman were prosecuted for manslaughter but they were found not guilty. The judge in his summing up bluntly concluded: "I could not but think that the railway company was seriously to blame for not having had in use a brake which not only was not the best in existence, but was known to be insufficient and liable to break down." With this damning rebuke the Manchester, Sheffield and Lincolnshire Railway, whose trains had been involved in both crashes, had no choice but to introduce continuous automatic braking.

But debates over which system was superior finally came to end in the aftermath of the Armagh accident in June 1889, where seventy-eight people, mainly children on a Sunday school outing were killed, and another 250 injured. The train had continuous brakes, but they were of the non-automatic vacuum type.

Here the brakes on the train failed as a gross over-crowded train struggled up an incline (see page 51). Such an accident coupled with the clear negligence of the railway company involved caused a huge public uproar.

Within weeks the Regulation of Railways Act was passed making companies introduce automatic continuous brakes on all passenger trains. O.S. Nock wrote that with the Act: "the fundamental principles of present day railway operating were attained and subsequent technical developments have tended towards the elimination of mistakes arising from the human element rather the establishment of new principles."

An additional benefit of continuous brakes was that they could be operated by passengers in case of an emergency by pulling a chain or handle. This assuaged a fear experienced by many Victorian passengers that they might be assaulted by strangers, without being able to raise the alarm.

Originally passenger carriages were little more than stagecoaches on bogies or, for unfortunate third-class passengers, waggons open to the elements. By leaps and bounds conditions improved helped by rigorous competition between the railways. But there were two major problems. Firstly the carriages remained light and flimsy. They were no stronger than a modern garden shed. This meant they were easy to haul, but if involved in a crash they could easily come off the rails and equally as easily be turned into matchsticks, as happened at Peasmarsh in 1873. A number of illustrations in this book show the spectacular fate of passenger carriages.

The answer lay in heavier steel-framed carriages designed to not buckle in case of an accident. However they were slow to be introduced.

One major problem until well into the twentieth century was that most carriages were lightly built out of wood, which meant that in a crash their passengers might have little chance of surviving. Here the Carriage Department at the Great Eastern works at Stratford are at work. Credit TNA RAIL 227/334 (4)

This photograph is of carriages smashed in the Dunbar crash of January 1898 in which one person was killed and twenty-one injured. At this time carriages were largely lit by gas which being very inflammable tended to ignite on sudden impact and spread rapidly. The fact that gas-lit carriages caught fire during the Quintinshill disaster of 1915 directly contributed to the huge loss of life. Credit SSPL 10624234

After the Harrow and Wealdstone crash on 8 October 1952, in which 112 people were killed, the inspector noted that the steel framed carriages had withstood the tremendous pressure well concluding: "It does seem possible, however, that the wreckage at Harrow might have been less compact, and the killed and injured fewer, if a greater proportion of the rolling stock had been of the latest all-steel type."

The other difficulty lay in lighting the carriages. Initially oil lamps were used, which were eventually replaced by gaslights. Both were very flammable. Many accidents were made worse by gas cylinders under the carriages fracturing and the gas catching fire. The worst example took place at Quintinshill on 22 May 1915, when about 226 people lost their lives – the worst railway accident by far in Britain. The tragedy was made worse because many of the carriages were very old and so lit by gas, caught fire. The gas escaping from cylinders ignited from the glowing coals from the engine of the troop train and soon everything was in flames. Those passengers who had not escaped were burnt to death. The train carried a number of fire extinguishers but inevitably they were unable to do very much.

It is little surprise that, in his recommendations, the Inspector Lieutenant Colonel E. Druitt suggested to prevent similar conflagrations in future:

> The construction of the coaches to be of steel as far as possible, with shock-absorbing buffers, and any timber or other combustible material used to be rendered non-inflammable. Special attention to be paid to the construction of the doorways, so that the doors shall not jam when a collision occurs [and] the provision of electric lighting in all new stock, and gas lighting in existing stock to be abolished and electric lighting to be provided as opportunity admits...

However good the machinery and the systems there is always the possibility of human error. An engine driver nods off, the signalman is distracted, or staff are just generally lax in their duties. As B.K. Cooper wrote in the introduction to O.S. Nock's *Historic Railway Disasters*: "Human error remains an imponderable and the reasons for it are often obscure. It has been a hazard for as long as there has been railways, whether caused by misunderstanding, lapses of attention or irresponsible conduct."

Sloppiness lay behind the accident at Abermule, in mid-Wales on 26 January 1921, which saw fifteen casualties and thirty-seven injuries, when an express train ran into the back of a stopping train at the station. Tom Rolt summed up the accident as "a classic example of the truth that no electrical or mechanical safety devices can altogether eliminate the human element: that in the first instance the safety of the travelling public must always depend upon the efficiency and vigilance of the railway staff."

Here lax working procedures allowed the safeguards provided by the electric-token system to be circumvented; a driver was handed a token for the wrong section, and proceeded on the mistaken belief the token was correct.

The tablet machines controlling the issuing of tokens or tablets permitting trains to enter single-track sections, were operated by any staff member who happened to be in the vicinity, instead of the stationmaster or the signalman, together with the failure of station staff to notify each other of their actions.

A contributory cause was the failure of anyone to examine the tablet they received by removing it from its pouch and checking it was the correct one. Since the system had worked faultlessly for years, it was being taken for granted. (See page 88)

It is a sobering thought that most railway accidents actually occur to railway staff rather than to the travelling public. In part they result from ignorance on part of both employers and employees. Often the Victorian railway companies refused to introduce basic safety equipment or procedures and made their staff work excessively long hours. In turn employees take short cuts or make silly mistakes. They ignore the rules, don't see oncoming trains and over-ride equipment.

Alcohol and machinery do not mix. Yet drunkenness was a particular problem on the early railway (as it was elsewhere in society at the time). In November 1838, William Paton of the London and Birmingham Railway wrote a letter describing a collision in which a ballast train was wrecked near Tring. In it he described how Stokes, the driver of one of the engines, managed to save his life by jumping on to the soft embankment. He was apparently "so much intoxicated he did not know the line he was on."

A less obvious, but more insidious problem, was tiredness. In the early years railway staff were expected to work long hours – twelve hours and more were not uncommon. A contributory factor to the Clayton Tunnel disaster in August 1861 was that Signalman Killick, who controlled the signals at the southern end of the tunnel, had been on duty for twenty-four hours, rather than the regulation eighteen, in order to gain a complete day off duty. In his report on the accident the Inspector Captain Tyler stated: "it was disgraceful that a man in so responsible a position as Signalman Killick should be compelled to work for twenty-four hours at a stretch in order to earn one day of rest a week." Here twenty-three people were killed and another 191 were seriously injured.

Tiredness was also clearly a contributory factor in the Bourne End accident eighty-five years later in September 1945. Driver Swaby and Fireman Jones were on the footplate of Royal Scots class No 6157 *Royal Artilleryman* as she pulled the very late running Perth Sleeper from Crewe to Euston. The train came off the rails going over points near Bourne End at sixty miles an hour – three times the speed she should have been going. The engine and seven carriages rolled down a short embankment killing forty-one passengers as well as the footplate crew. Either the footplate crew had ignored or had not seen warning signals telling them to slow down. In the weeks before the accident Swaby and his partner had volunteered to undertake extra duties for other men or to the make up the shortage of trained staff as the result of wartime conditions. This meant they had worked for nearly a month without a break. In concluding his investigation into the accident the Inspector Sir Alan Mount noted: "The action of certain men in not making themselves available for rostered and agreed service on Sundays must have resulted in greater strain being borne by others."

Railway staff could also have other issues affecting their performance. The immediate cause of the accident at Norton Fitzwarren on 11 November 1890, in which ten people were killed, was that the signalman George Rice had forgotten a goods train was still on the main line after being shunted, and allowed the boat train into his section with the line obstructed. He contributed his poor performance to having been knocked down by a light engine in the

In the early days staff were often drunk when on duty. This posed many dangers to both the staff themselves and the passengers, whose care they were responsible for. In this letter about an accident at Tring on the line between London and Birmingham, Driver Stokes saved his life by jumping on to the soft embankment. He was apparently "so much intoxicated he did not know the line he was on." Credit RAIL 384/280

previous January and had not fully recovered. He told the Inspector he had been "bad in the head" the whole evening. In fact the pain was "worse than usual".

A major crash occurred at Manor House near Thirsk on 2 November 1892. It resulted from errors made by the signalman James Holmes, who permitted a goods train to remain on the line while the Scotch Express was expected. Nine passengers and the guard of the goods train were killed, and thirty-nine people injured. At Holmes' trial for manslaughter it was revealed that the day before the crash, his baby daughter Rose was taken ill and later died. As might be expected Holmes was extremely distressed and had been awake for thirty-six hours, ministering to the child, walking miles trying to find the local doctor and comforting his distraught wife. He reported to the stationmaster at Otterington that he would be unable to work the shift on the next night, but the stationmaster merely asked his superiors for a relief signalman, without stating the reason why Holmes had reported himself unfit to work. As a result, no relief signalman was appointed and James was forced to work his shift.

Holmes was found guilty, but given an absolute discharge to public acclaim. The North Eastern Railway, his employers, were roundly criticised for not supplying a relief signalman in such as situation. (see page 69)

It wasn't just on the rails accidents could and did occur to staff. There were also workshops, train sheds and carriage depots where it was easy for men to injure themselves. Many more injuries and deaths occurred here then on passenger or freight trains.

Most were fairly trivial. The accident book of the London Chatham and Dover Railway includes many such incidents. In November 1882, for example, Engineman George Hibbert lost two fingers, which were caught between the block and the engine when the fireman unexpectedly applied the brake wheel. A few years later, in July 1887, Fireman W.G. Foster had his head cut and body bruised after falling into the pit at Battersea Shed. And lastly on New Year's Eve 1888 Engineman J. Coventry was struck on the back of his head with a bottle thrown from the 5.30pm boat train while he was oiling an engine at Victoria.

The most serious accidents tended to occur in the workshops and engine sheds. In his classic account of the Great Western Railway works at Swindon *Life in a Railway Factory*, published in 1915, Alfred Williams describes how dangerous work could be, but also the fatalistic mind-set of the men themselves:

As soon as a serious accident happens to a workman a rush is made to the spot by young and old alike – they cannot contain their eager curiosity and excitement. Many are impelled by a strong desire to be of service to the unfortunate individual who has been hurt, though, in nine cases out of ten, instead of being a help they are a very great hindrance. If the workman is injured very severely, or if he happens to be killed, it will be impossible to keep the crowd back; in spite of commands and exhortations they use their utmost powers to approach the spot and catch a glimpse of the victim. The overseer shouts, curses, and waves his hands frantically, and warns them all of what he will do, but

Most accidents occurred (and still occur) to railway personnel. The railway companies increasingly endeavoured to train their staff in how to avoid accidents. Here a team of gangers on the Great Western seemingly demonstrate how to run over a colleague with a trolley. Credit STEAM A2/048

the men doggedly refuse to disperse until they have satisfied their curiosity and abated their excitement.

The GWR, and the other railway companies, increasingly did their best to encourage safety and to provide first aid where appropriate. There were notices and safeguards on dangerous

It was easy enough for a cleaner cleaning the windows of a carriage to step back and lose his balance. This was one of a number of posed photographs taken and posted up in mess rooms and other places where staff of the Great Western Railway assembled as a reminder to be careful. Credit STEAM A2/052

machinery. Each of the works had first aid teams and regular exercises to practice dealing with emergencies. And many had special accident trains ready to go to the site of any crash in order to clear the wreckage.

Today railways are much, much safer than travelling by car. At the time of writing the last passenger to be killed in a rail accident was in 2008. During 2010/11 three people died getting on and off trains (or "at the platform-train interface" in the terminology) and another falling off an escalator. And one railway employee "died in a road traffic accident while on duty". In 2010/11 252 passengers were seriously injured out of a total of 1.5 billion journeys made by rail. Even more remarkable, bearing in mind railways have always been inherently dangerous places to work, there were just 152 serious injuries to railway staff.

By contrast, 1901 men, women and children were killed on the roads during the same period and another 220,000 casualties were reported to the police during the year. If such large numbers of casualties occurred on the railways, nobody would travel by them. The reasons are as Charles Adams observed in the 1870s: "Every one rode behind horses... and when disaster came it involved but a few persons and was rarely accompanied by circumstances which neither struck the imagination or attracted any great public notice." The horseless carriage may have replaced the horse, but the arguments remain the same.

And although this book may suggest otherwise, the fact is, as Charles Adams noted: "It is not, after all, the dangers but the safety of the modern railroad which should excite our special wonder."

The larger railway companies had an Accident Train prepared to be sent to accident locations to clear debris and repair track and other infrastructure. This is the set maintained by the Great Eastern Railway photographed at the Stratford Depot in February 1910. Credit TNA RAIL 227/434 (1)

Accidents were very common in workshops and engineering shops. The railway companies provided varying degrees of help for their employees who were injured in the course of their duties. Here a first aid team at the works in Swindon demonstrate how to use a rather complicated looking stretcher. Credit STEAM s37a A/021

Chapter One

Accidents on the Early Railway 1829–1889

At first sight this accident at Barrs Court near Hereford on 20 August 1858 would have led to many casualties. However as the train was moving so slowly when the engine jumped the points and pulled the carriages down the embankment with it, no passengers were hurt although local newspapers reported they were all rather shaken up. Credit SSPL 10624236

The *Actaeon* after her boiler had exploded at Gloucester station on 7 February 1855. Nobody was killed in the accident. The inspector concluded that the boiler was too old and should have been replaced. The locomotive had been built as long ago as 1841. **Credit STEAM A 1/009**

The "ACTAEON,"
JOHN BROWN, Driver.

The boiler of this engine exploded, in Glo'ster Station yard, close to the water tank, on February 7th, 1855.

A photographic montage of the scene of the accident. **Credit** SSPL 10323041

The track was being renovated at Staplehurst, Kent where it crossed on a low cast-iron girder bridge over the River Beult. The timing of the Folkestone Boat Express, varied with the tides, which governed the arrival of ships at the port. On 9 June 1865, the foreman mistakenly believed that the train would arrive later than it did, and the final two rails had not yet been replaced. The foreman posted a lookout, but he was not far enough away to adequately warn the fast-approaching train. Detonators should have been placed on the rails as an additional safeguard, but they also were missing. Ten people were killed in the accident and another forty injured many seriously. Among the passengers was Charles Dickens, who was returning from the Continent with his mistress Ellen Terry and her mother. Uninjured himself he helped the wounded, but was subsequently traumatised by the crash.

SCENE OF THE FATAL ACCIDENT AT STAPLEHURST, ON THE SOUTH-EASTERN RAILWAY.—FROM A SKETCH TAKEN NEXT DAY.

A scene of the crash as it appeared in the *Illustrated London News*. **Credit** TNA RAIL ZPER 34/46

happens in cases of accident that the amount of break-power upon a train makes all the difference of life or death to the passengers. In this particular instance, there was (leaving the 1,100 yards from the green flag to where the platelayers were working out of the question) a clear 600 yards for the application of break-power after the leading engine left the rails with two of its wheels. And a sufficient amount of break-power applied to the carriages over that distance would have caused them to act as a drag upon the engines instead of forcing them forward, and have so far reduced the speed that the great destruction of carriages which took place would have been prevented, and probably no lives would have been lost, when the carriages were finally brought to a stand.

Having reference to the present accident, as well as to that which has recently occurred with such lamentable results on another railway, I would observe, in conclusion, that whenever it is necessary, in consequence of an alteration in the permanent way of a railway, or from any other cause, to warn the engine-driver of a train at a point where there are no fixed signals, it is desirable that explosive (commonly called fog) signals should invariably be employed in addition to those hand signals—flags by day and lamps by night—which are too frequently used alone on such occasions. An engine-driver, properly acquainted with the line on which he is running, knows where the fixed signals are situated, and exactly the points at which he ought to look for them; and he is less liable to miss seeing those signals; but he is not, though he ought always to be on the look-out, so sure to catch sight of an unexpected flag or lamp at the proper moment. Travelling at high speed, perhaps at 30, perhaps even at 60 miles an hour, or, in other words, at from half a mile to a mile in a minute, he may, during a glance at his fire, or his gauges, or at some portion of the machinery of his engine, omit to observe a flag at the side of the line, or a man in front of him at a point where he would not expect to find the permanent way obstructed.

The servants of a company in charge of the permanent way may be compelled to replace damaged or broken materials at any moment, in order to secure the safety of the traffic; but it is incumbent upon them, under the printed rules which are in force upon the different railways, to exhibit a warning signal when the line is not safe for traffic at the speeds ordinarily employed, not only to a train that may be expected, but also to any train that may approach them without notice. It is necessary, for the reasons above given, that they should, in doing so, appeal, by the use of explosive signals, to the sense of hearing as well as to the sense of sight of the engine-drivers, in order to ensure their obeying a signal thus made to them on a part of the line where they may not expect to find it.

I have, &c.
H. W. TYLER,
Capt. R.E.

The Secretary
Board of Trade,
Whitehall.

SOUTH-EASTERN RAILWAY.

Board of Trade
(Railway Department),
Whitehall, 22nd June 1865.

SIR,

I AM directed by the Lords of the Committee of Privy Council for Trade to transmit to you, to be laid before the Directors of the South-Eastern Railway Company, the enclosed copy of the report made by Captain Rich, R.E., the officer appointed by their Lordships to inquire into the circumstances connected with the accident which occurred, on the 9th instant, to the tidal passenger train near Staplehurst on the South-Eastern Railway.

My Lords trust that the Directors will give the recommendations contained in Captain Rich's report their careful consideration.

I am, &c.
JAMES BOOTH.

The Secretary of the
South-Eastern
Railway Company.

SIR,
Dulwich, 21st June 1865.

IN compliance with the instructions contained in your letter of the 10th instant, I have the honour to report, for the information of the Lords of the Committee of Privy Council for Trade, the result of my inquiry into the circumstances which attended the lamentable accident that occurred on the 9th instant, near Staplehurst station, on the South-Eastern railway, by which 10 persons were killed and 40 others injured, some of them very seriously.

It appears that a gang of 4 carpenters, one laborer, and 3 platelayers, all of whom worked under the direction of the foreman of platelayers, has been employed for the last 8 or 10 weeks in taking out and renewing the longitudinal timbers that carry the rails on three viaducts, situated to the east of Staplehurst Station.

It was deemed expedient to execute these repairs during the intervals when the line would not be required for passenger traffic, rather than stop the traffic on one line, and turn the whole traffic over a single line. The repairs, executed as they were one length at a time, (the new baulk always being fitted, ready for inserting, before the rail was disturbed,) could have been executed easily and safely, at properly selected intervals.

As the baulks had to be fitted ready for inserting before disturbing the road, it was desirable and necessary for the man on the spot who was in charge of the work to select these intervals. The platelayer or foreman of the gang, under whose orders all the carpenters and other platelayers were working, was that person. He bears the character of being a very steady and intelligent man, has been employed by the South-Eastern Railway Company 10 years, and has acted for 2 years and 10 months as foreman of platelayers on the two miles of road where the repairs were being executed.

His daily presence on this length of road must have given him a thorough knowledge of the times when all trains were due, except the tidal train; and he must have been equally aware that the time when the tidal train passed was always changing. The time service table that was furnished to him, that he had in his possession, and was seen to refer to, on the morning of the unfortunate calamity, afforded him the necessary information as to the time the tidal train would pass.

When at breakfast on the morning of the 9th inst. he informed some of the men sitting near him that the tidal train would not pass till 5.20 p.m. that day. He had the time service book in his hand at the time, and was seen to refer to it, but he mistook the time the tidal train would be due at Headcorn on the 10th June, for the time that it was due on the 9th, and read the time as 5.20 p.m. instead of 3.15 p.m., about which time it arrived.

The leading carpenter was also supplied with a time service book, but it had been cut in two, by a wheel passing over it, and as he was working under the orders of the foreman of platelayers, who had a

F 4

A page of the HM Railway Inspector's report into the Staplehurst crash. Captain Rich found that the foreman of the railway had been negligent and recommended that he be prosecuted for manslaughter. Credit TNA RAIL 1053/57, p41

On 5 November 1868, the 5pm Mail Train from Milford Haven pulled by *Rob Roy* ran into the rear of a cattle train near Newnham on the Severn estuary, causing the locomotive to over-ride two cattle wagons. Three drovers and the guard were killed on the cattle train. The cattle train had stalled on the gradient due to bad rail adhesion. Both trains were working on a Time Interval System of approximately twenty-minute intervals but owing to the continued problem with the cattle train the mail had caught up and collided with it. The Inspectorate recommended that block signalling be introduced on the line. This photograph shows the location of the crash and the locomotive *Rob Roy* which had been pulling the Mail Train. Note the broad gauge track used by the Great Western until 1892. **Credit STEAM A/005**

A wreckage crew swarms over *Rob Roy* preparing to move the locomotive from the track. The smartly dressed chief engineer W.G. Owen in the top hat supervises their work. **Credit STEAM A/006**

A bizarre coincidence occurred at Friog near Fairbourne on the Aberystwyth and Welsh Coat Railway. On 1 January 1883, and then again fifty years later in 1933, a rock fall knocked a locomotive off the tracks and down onto the beach. In both cases no passengers were hurt. This view shows locomotive No22 *Pegasus* on the beach with a carriage on the cliff. The footplate men were killed. *Pegasus* was rebuilt and was in service for a further thirty years. **Credit STEAM A1/087**

Tay Bridge Disaster 28 December 1879

The Tay Bridge disaster occurred during a violent storm on the evening of 28 December 1879. The bridge collapsed while a train was passing over it from Wormit to Dundee, killing all seventy-five passengers and crew.

The subsequent inquiry found that the Bridge by Sir Thomas Bouche had been badly designed – he had seriously underestimated the strength of the winds that blew down the Tay. In addition the bridge had been badly maintained and witnesses reported that it shook as trains crossed it, particularly on the northbound track.

Bouche died in disgrace a few months later. A new bridge, much strengthened, opened to traffic in 1887. Passengers can observe the stumps of the old bridge as they cross the Tay. Surprisingly there does not appear to be a memorial to those who lost their lives.

The *Illustrated London News* shows a bilious looking Queen Victoria crossing the Tay Bridge a few months before the disaster.
Credit TNA ZPER 34/75

Boats try in vain to find survivors. Only forty-six bodies were recovered, two of which were not found until the following February. **Credit TNA ZPER 34/76 (1)**

The wreckage of the Bridge photographed a few days after the disaster. Credit SSPL 10624243

A bizarre montage showing some of the tickets purchased by the passengers on the ill-fated train across the Tay Bridge. **Credit TNA COPY 1/373**

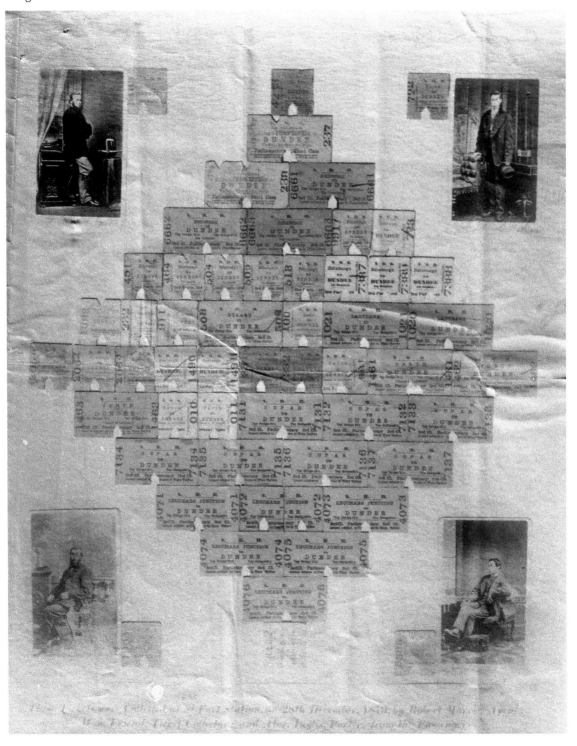

Armagh 12 June 1889

A crowded Sunday school excursion train full of local children negotiated a steep incline; the steam locomotive was unable to complete the climb and the train stalled. The train crew decided to divide the train and take forward the front portion, leaving the rear portion on the running line. The rear portion was inadequately braked and ran back down the gradient, colliding with a following train. Eighty people were killed and 260 injured, about a third of them children. It was the worst rail disaster in Europe during the nineteenth century, and remains Ireland's worst railway disaster ever.

The subsequent inquiry found that a host of mistakes and confusions coupled with bad management led up to the accident. But worst of all the Great Northern Railway of Ireland persisted in using an inferior form of vacuum breaking which could not prevent the carriages from running away. The death of so many children led to a public outcry and Parliament speedily passed legislation forcing railway companies to improve the safety of their trains.

Many of the children were buried in mass graves in St Mary's churchyard, Armagh.

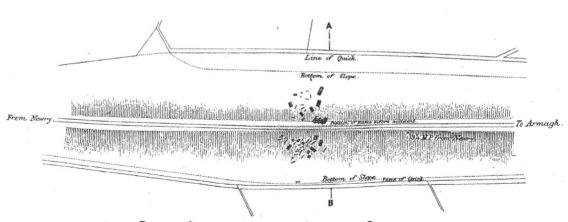

PLAN OF LINE AT AND NEAR SCENE OF COLLISION.

Scale 40 feet to an Inch.

A plan from the official report showing the scene of the crash and where the carriages ended up. **Credit Taylor Collection**

Rescuers and onlookers at the site of the crash near Armagh. **Credit TNA COPY 1/396 (1)**

A view of the crash site showing some of the debris. Credit TNA COPY 1/396 (2)

An engraving from the *Illustrated London News* entitled 'Extracting the Dead and Wounded'. One of the worst head-on collisions in British railway history occurred on 10 September 1874, at Thorpe between Brundall and Norwich stations, when two trains were mistakenly despatched from either end of the single line, killing twenty-five people and injuring seventy-five. Although the accident was caused by human error, the Inspector criticised the laxity of the system that permitted such a mistake to occur. **Credit: SSPL 10315739**

RAILWAY AMALGAMATION—A PLEASANT STATE OF THINGS

Passenger. "What's the matter, guard?"

Guard (with presence of mind). "Oh, nothing particular, sir. We've only run into an excursion train!"

Passenger. "But, good gracious! there's a train just behind us, isn't there?"

Guard. "Yes, sir! But a boy has gone down the line with a signal; and it's very likely they'll see it!"

An early *Punch* cartoon commenting on railway crashes. Many accidents were caused by the time interval working system where by trains were despatched at agreed intervals. If a train broke down or was delayed there was almost no way of preventing another train running into it. **Credit Mr Punch's Railway Book**

On 16 September 1887, a Liverpool to Hull express train crashed into the back of another train standing at Hexthorpe Station, carrying race goers to the St Leger meeting at nearby Doncaster. There were twenty-five killed and sixty-six injured, most of the casualties being passengers on the stationary train. The accident was remarkable because all the employees of the Manchester, Sheffield and Lincolnshire Railway, which ran both trains, offered to forego a day's pay in order to defray the costs of the disaster. Their offer was declined with thanks. The picture used by the *Illustrated London News* is taken from a sketch by an eyewitness, Walter J. Stuart, and shows the dead and wounded being extricated from the wreckage of the accident. **Credit SSPL 10317915**

Chapter Two

The Golden Age of the Railway Accident 1890–1914

With safety effectively regulated by the Board of Trade the number of accidents began to fall. However, there were still a number of spectacular crashes, which were recorded for posterity by a generation of photographers using fairly portable equipment. This meant that for the first time professional photographers could bring their cameras to take close up shots of the wreckage. And there was money to be made from selling photographs as souvenirs or turned into picture postcards. These souvenirs fed a seemingly insatiable market for destruction, which was only cured by the First World War.

One striking thing about these photographs is the number of onlookers to be found in the margins of each shot. Any railway accident - particularly the larger ones - would attract them. Such crashes, as they often referred to, would have been a big event particularly in small villages. A study of their clothes show they come from all social classes. And what is surprising to modern eyes is the number of children who appear in many shots, either with their nannies or parents or who were the local village scallywags.

The Norton Fitzwarren accident took place in the early hours of 11 November 1890. A special boat train carrying passengers from Plymouth to Paddington collided with a goods train that was being shunted on the main line. Ten passengers were killed, and eleven people (including the driver and fireman of the boat train) were seriously injured. Here you can see through a carefully posed shot of the mangled goods engine with onlookers (note the boys) and a local policeman. Credit TNA COPY 1/402

On 9 January 1892 five people were killed and a further thirty injured as Esholt Junction near Guiseley, Yorkshire. Two trains collided at the Junction when an Ilkley-bound train ploughed through the last six carriages of the Bradford-bound train, overturning the last of these; the engine and tender of the Ilkley-bound train also turned over. Although vegetation obscuring a signal was accepted as the primary cause of the crash, the Inspector recommended that signalling procedures at the Junction be changed to prevent a recurrence. **Credit TNA COPY 1/409**

The 1890s and 1900s had some very severe winter weather particularly in Scotland, which affected the railways. At worst trains could get completely snowed in. Here a Highland Railway locomotive is trying to free itself from snow near Helmsdale in January 1895. **Credit TNA COPY 1/419**

The results of the crash at Preston station at 12.15am on 13 July 1896 with the derailed locomotives 2159 *Shark* in the foreground and 275 *Vulcan* in the middle ground. The derailment occurred when a driver sped through a 10mph restriction at the north end of the station at 45mph in order to maintain a tight schedule on an express train between Euston and Glasgow. According to O.S. Nock the results were spectacular indeed: "the leading engine jumped the rails; but instead of turning over it went straight on, leapfrogging over the intervening tracks to finish still standing bolt upright within a short distance of a retaining wall over which there was a 20ft drop into a works yard." Despite the devastation only one passenger was killed. The Inspector suggested that the station be rebuilt to remove the speed restriction. More importantly public fears over excessive speeds led to an end of the great race between the London and North Western and Great Northern railways to Scotland and a general increase in journey times. **Credit TNA COPY 1/425**

Another accident occurred at Preston a few weeks after the major crash on 13 July. The accident shown here took place at Preston Junction late on Bank Holiday Monday, 3 August 1896, when a late-running train from Blackpool collided with a train waiting to go into the station. There was one fatality. **Credit SSPL 10624240**

Little Bytham on the Lincolnshire/Rutland border is famous among rail enthusiasts as being the spot where in July 1938 A4 4468 *Mallard* reached the highest speed achieved by a steam locomotive of 126mph. However on 3 March 1896 No 1003 pulling an express train between Leeds and London was derailed here with the loss of two lives. **Credit SSPL 10624237**

The accident at Little Bytham saw carriages fall off the viaduct which goes through the village. Here villagers inspect the damage. The cause of the accident was probably due to a fault in the design of the locomotive No 1003 as there had been two other similar accidents in previous months involving the same class of engines. Credit SSPL 10624238

The damage to this carriage occurred at March, Cambridgeshire on 23 September 1896 when an express between Harwich and York collided with an excursion train to Hunstanton. One passenger was killed and another twenty-one injured. According to the *Manchester Guardian*: "A scene of intense excitement and terror arose, some of the passengers screaming for help." **Credit TNA COPY 1/427**

Work gangs clear-up after an accident at Wellingborough on 2 September 1898. Seven people were killed and sixty-five injured when an express between St Pancras and Manchester collided with a luggage trolley that had fallen on the track. Despite frantic efforts by staff and a group of small boys at the station they were unable to remove it in time. **Credit SSPL 10624246**

A view of the boiler of locomotive No 1743 after the accident at Wellingborough. As with most engines involved in crashes it was too expensive to scrap, so it was rebuilt and re-entered service. **Credit SSPL 10624247**

Nº1   The Wreck of the Scotch Express. 1892 – NEAR THIRSK

Firemen inspect the remains of the wreckage of the accident at Manor House near Thirsk on 2 November 1892. The crash resulted from errors made by the signalman James Holmes, who permitted a goods train to remain on the line while the *Scotch Express* was expected. As a result the *Express* crashed at 60mph into the goods train. Nine passengers and the guard of the goods train were killed, and thirty-nine people injured. Holmes was later tried for manslaughter where the tragedy of his personal life, which lay behind the mistakes he made, was revealed. **Credit SSPL** 10624235

North British Railway engine No 642 after the accident at Dunbar on 3 January 1898. Driver Steedman on the Night Express between London and Edinburgh passed a signal at danger and having realised his mistake was unable to slow down in time and thus collided with goods wagons which were being moved across the mainline. One person was killed and twenty-three injured. **Credit SSPL 10624233**

This derailment at Penmaenmawr on the North Wales line took place on 13 January 1899. Winter storms had washed away part of the embankment. The driver of a goods train lost his life as he walked towards an oncoming passenger train to warn it of the damage to the line. **Credit COPY 1/439 f366**

Officials inspect the damage caused by the derailment of the 09:27 London Liverpool Street to Cromer express at Witham. The crash was caused by platelayers failing to replace a crossover in time. **Credit SSPL 10624252**

A view of one of the carriages at Witham station. Ten passengers and a luggage porter were killed when several of the carriages somersaulted on to the platforms causing considerable damage to the rolling stock and the station. In addition seventy-one passengers were seriously injured. Credit SSPL 10624251

Not all accidents by any means involved passenger trains. This one at Brocklesby near Immingham on 27 March 1907 involved a goods train taking fish from Grimsby to Yorkshire. Two people were injured. **Credit SSPL 10446524**

COLLISION AT BROCKLESBY 27 MAR 1907 SCENE ON PLATFORM 406

The Great Western Railway was regarded with some justification as being the safest of railways. Initially this was because of the greater stability offered by the 7 feet wide broad gauge, but when this was phased out in the 1880s and 1890s the safety record remained almost as good. One of the very few blemishes was this crash between Loughor and Llanelli on 3 October 1904 in which five people were killed and ninety-four injured as the result of a derailment of a train from New Milford. The cause of the derailment was never discovered by the Inspector. Credit TNA COPY 1/478

In the early hours of 23 December 1904 at Aylesbury one of the most dramatic of railway accidents occurred. Fortunately there were only four fatalities and four injuries. Lieutenant Colonel H.A. Yorke of the Railway Inspectorate commented: "So far as the destruction of rolling stock is concerned, this is probably one of the worst cases of derailment that has occurred in the United Kingdom. Of the ten coaches forming the train, six were entirely, and one partially, demolished." Our view is of the Great Central Railway locomotive No 1040 which was pulling a night express from Marylebone to Manchester. Despite what appears in the photograph the engine was actually only superficially damaged. **Credit TNA COPY 1/481**

The causes of some accidents will never be known. At 11pm there was consternation at Grantham as the 08.43pm train from London Kings Cross for Edinburgh failed to stop. Worse was to follow as the train veered off onto the branch line to Nottingham and eventually the carriages toppled over and the engine and remaining carriages crashed into a bridge. The train was almost entirely wrecked. Fourteen were killed (including Driver Fleetwood and Fireman Talbot). Without these key witnesses the Inspector was unable to ascertain why they did as they did. The photograph shows the wreckage being removed a day or two later. **Credit TNA COPY 1/501**

On 4 February 1909 Driver Arthur Coope and Fireman John Hawley lost their lives in an accident as their goods train collided with a stationary train at Sharnbrook near Bedford. The crash is commemorated in this picture postcard. Although the crash was serious it certainly did not warrant treatment of this kind. **Credit COPY 1/515**

Less speed more haste might be the lesson of the crash at Salisbury on 1 July 1906. Driver Robins and Fireman Gadd were in charge of the weekly boat train which took passengers from the Atlantic liners at Plymouth to London. There was great competition for this lucrative trade between the Great Western and London and South Western railways. So Robins and Gadd, of the LSWR, knew that they had to keep to time as they sped at seventy miles an hour through a thirty miles an hour section to the east of Salisbury station. Disaster struck as the engine and carriages came off the rails. Considerable damage was done as this photograph shows with twenty-four passengers losing their lives along with the train crew. **Credit SSPL 10624241**

THE RAILWAY DISASTER AT SALISBURY, JULY. 1ST, 1906.
F. FUTCHER, PHOTO. 10, FISHERTON ST.

On 25 September 1900 the boiler of Great Eastern Railway locomotive 522 exploded at Westerfield station just north of Ipswich killing the driver and fireman, demolishing the level crossing gatekeeper's cottage and slightly injuring two passers-by a policeman and a newspaper boy. The Inspector found that the explosion was probably caused by a lack of water in the boiler – the fault had been previously identified and various attempts had been made to repair it. Judging by the crowds the explosion was the most exciting thing to happen in the village for many a long day! **Credit TNA RAIL 243/434 (5)**

No accident seems to have occurred at Tharston Bridge near Forncett in Norfolk at the end of August 1912. The bridge had been washed away by severe flooding. Here men from the Great Eastern Railway survey the problem before undertaking repairs. Credit TNA RAIL 243/434 (3)

This is perhaps the most dramatic photograph of a railway accident ever taken. An unknown photographer took this shot of a steam locomotive at Montparnasse Station in Paris. The local train from Granville went through the buffers and crashed through the station wall into the street below. **Credit SSPL** 10428570

Chapter Three

The Years of War and Peace 1914–1947

The period of the two world wars and the twenty-year gap between them was a traumatic one for British railways. There were the stresses and strains of the world wars which saw more traffic than ever use the rails carrying munitions, troops and supplies on ever more battered tracks. In 1923, what became known as the Grouping, saw the amalgamation of almost all railway companies into just four. But the efficiencies that this offered were increasingly not enough to fend off competition from buses, lorries and the private motor car. Encouraged by still emotive posters there is a tendency to see the Interwar period as a Golden Age with streamlined express trains, but this hides increasingly serious problems with investment on the permanent way and new trains. And, as a result, there were a number of serious accidents.

The railway accident at Quintinshill near Gretna Green on 22 May 1915 was the worst to have occurred on British rails. It involved five trains, killed probably 230 passengers and injured 246. Those killed were mainly Territorial soldiers from the 1/7th (Leith) Battalion, the Royal Scots heading for Gallipoli. The precise number of dead was never established with confidence as the regiment's muster roll was destroyed in the fire.

The crash occurred when a troop train travelling from Larbert to Liverpool collided with a local passenger train that had been shunted on to the main line, to then be hit by an express train to Glasgow which crashed into the wreckage a minute later. Gas from the lighting system of the old wooden carriages of the troop train ignited, starting a fire which soon engulfed the three passenger trains and also two goods trains standing on nearby passing loops. The immediate cause was the sloppy working practices of the local signalmen, which led to their imprisonment for culpable homicide. The only railway workers ever to be so punished.

The picture shows part of the funeral procession in Edinburgh carrying some of the victims to their last resting place in the city's Rosebank cemetery. **Credit Wikicommons**

Many of the carriages carrying troops at Quitinshill were made of wood and lit by gas. In almost any circumstance they were a fire hazard. And although there were fire extinguishers in each carriage they proved almost useless.
Credit Author/The Graphic

A view of the derailed locomotive under Penistone Viaduct on the Lancashire & Yorkshire Railway on 2 February 1916. This accident was caused because part of the viaduct had collapsed when heavy rain weakened the foundations. The driver and fireman of the freight locomotive jumped clear and survived the crash. Credit SSPL 10446498

A collision occurred at Abermule station in mid-Wales on 26 January 1921 resulting in the deaths of seventeen people, including Lord Herbert Vane-Tempest, one of the directors of the Cambrian Railways which operated the line. Another thirty-six passengers were injured.

The incident saw a very rare head-on crash. It arose from misunderstandings between staff who effectively over-rode the safe operation of the Electric Train Tablet system protecting the single line. A train departed carrying the wrong tablet for the section it was entering and collided with a train coming the other way. By the time the mistake had been realised it was too late to prevent the collision.

A view of the wrecked trains at Abermule. Credit Railway Archives

Workmen clear wreckage from the line at Abermule a day or so after the accident. There is a clip on *YouTube* showing the aftermath of the collision. **Credit STEAM A 1/084**

On 21 January 1941 London Midland and Scottish locomotive 8247 tumbled from the rails at Wallneuk Junction, Paisley into a drained canal. The engine was rescued, rebuilt and continued in service until the end of steam on British Railways in August 1968. **Credit SSPL 10624245**

At about 10.52am on 10 February 1941 a stopping train to Southend ploughed into the rear of an express train between London and Norwich near Brentwood. The express had run short of steam after ascending the steep Brentwood bank and had been stationary for a few minutes when the accident happened. Seven people were killed and another ninety-nine were injured, although most injuries were minor. The picture shows the engine of the Southend train telescoped into the rear of the Norwich express. **Credit SSPL 10553033**

An accident to Great Western Steam Railcar No 91 at Cropredy, Oxfordshire at an unknown date. Some ninety-nine steam-powered railcars, designed by George Jackson Churchward, were built for the Great Western Railway before the First World War. They were designed for use on the less busy branch lines. Eventually they were converted for use by diesel motive power. The cars were gradually withdrawn from service in the 1920s. Railcar No 93 has been preserved and is being renovated at Didcot Railway Centre. **Credit STEAM A1/083**

In the early hours of 2 July 1941 the Plymouth to Paddington express collided with a freight train at Dolphin Junction near Slough station. Five passengers were killed, including three naval ratings, and another twenty-four were injured. The cause was an error by the signalman allowing the express onto the down line occupied by the freight. **Credit STEAM: Harry's Slough 1941**

Crowds examine a carriage which had telescoped into the freight train at Dolphin Junction in July 1941. **Credit STEAM: Harry's possible Slough 1941 3**

It is easy to forget that the quick thinking and heroism of railway workers have prevented many accidents or reduced the effect of others. This is nowhere more true than at Soham on 2 June 1944 when a fire developed on the leading wagon of a heavy ammunition train as it was entering the Cambridgeshire village. The wagon contained a quantity of high explosive bombs. The train crew had detached the wagon from the rest of the train and were drawing it away when the cargo exploded. The fireman of the train and the signalman at Soham signalbox were killed and several other people injured. Driver, Benjamin Gimbert, and Fireman, James Nightall, were both awarded the George Cross for their bravery. Undoubtedly the village would have been destroyed with great loss of life had they not moved the wagon. As it was the explosion created a crater 66-feet in diameter and 15-feet deep, the station buildings were almost demolished and there was severe or moderate damage to over 700 properties within half a mile radius of the explosion. In the photograph American servicemen from a nearby base help clear the wreckage. Remarkably the line was in operation again less than eighteen hours after the accident. Credit SSPL 10624242

Great Western locomotive 6001 *King Edward VII* gingerly crosses over a repaired embankment near Bath early in the Second World War with a track-measuring coach. **Credit: STEAM A2/010**

A crane helps upright a stricken locomotive "somewhere in England" during the Second World War. **Credit: STEAM A2/072**

Chapter Four

Accidents on British Railways 1948–1968

The railways were finally nationalised on 1 January 1948. The new British Railways inherited massive problems, particularly as the system had been starved of investment for many years. This lack of investment hampered the introduction of new safety and warning systems. The Automatic Warning System was adopted by British Railways in 1956 to warn drivers of danger signals ahead, but it was slow to roll out across the whole system. Even so the railways remained a very safe place on which to travel despite a number of high profile accidents, notably the crash at Harrow and Wealdstone in October 1952 which saw the deaths of 112 passengers and the Lewisham disaster of December 1957 when ninety people were killed.

The age of steam finally ended in August 1968. Although dull and unromantic to most enthusiasts, diesels and electric trains were designed from the start with safety in mind. And with continuing improvements fatal accidents on the railways are now very rare.

Small boys look on eagerly as the wreckage of the Aberdonian Express south of Welwyn Garden City is cleared away. The accident occurred on 7 January 1957 when the Express ploughed into a slow train on the line into London. One passenger was killed and another forty-four injured. The driver of the Aberdonian had ignored the signals and explosive warning devices placed on the track by signalmen at Welwyn. **Credit © Ben Brooksbank and licensed for reuse under this Creative Commons Licence**

The view South West from Brookmill Road near Lewisham station, three days after the collision at 18.20 on 4 December 1957 in dense fog, when the Cannon Street to Ramsgate express collided with a waiting train at St John's Station with such force that the massive bridge fly-over carrying the Nunhead – Lewisham line was brought down onto the leading coaches of the express. In this picture the damaged bridge is being cut up to clear the lines and allow the removal of the parts of the train caught under the collapsed bridge. Incidentally the temporary structure that replaced the bridge is still in use today. **Credit © Ben Brooksbank and licensed for reuse under this Creative Commons Licence**

On 18 September 1953 the 3.12pm train from Waterloo ran into the buffers at Guildford station. The official accident report noted that: "the first coach was dislodged from its bogies and was shot forward over the platform. It demolished the end wall of the station building and then passed through the Station Master's personal office, his Clerk's office and the Enquiry Lobby, finally coming to rest when the buffers hit the wall of the Fish Store alongside the Parcels Office. The front of the second coach was lifted off its leading bogie and was driven against the coach ahead, but the rest of the train remained on the rails." Remarkably only two passengers and five station staff were injured. **Credit TNA MT 114/54**

A commuter train outside Woking station was struck on the evening on 23 December 1955 by the London to Bournemouth Express. Nobody was killed although twenty-one passengers suffered minor injuries. Here the electric commuter train and the express are being examined by railway engineering staff for damage. **Credit TNA MT 114/58**

The last two carriages of 6.52am train from Sanderstead to London Cannon Street station on 8 August 1960 became derailed because of worn points. Fortunately nobody was seriously hurt. **Credit** TNA MT 114/291

Due to a signalling error between Knowle and Dorridge on 8 August 1963 the Birmingham to Paddington express ran into a freight train which was being shunted along the line. The driver, the co-driver and a fireman of the express were killed. No passengers were hurt. **Credit TNA MT 114/481**

On 8 July 1961 an express train from Colne to Fleetwood collided with an engineer's ballast wagon near Weeton. The signalman at nearby Singleton station misunderstood a telephone message which led him to make a serious error and he wrongly accepted the diesel train. Six passengers and the driver of the express lost their lives and 116 passengers were injured. In this photograph passengers are being escorted from the train to safety.
Credit SSPL 10455116

Carriages tower over the scene of the collision at Weeton on 8 July 1961. **Credit SSPL 10455123**

Even freight trains could get into trouble. Here engine 4707 has come off the track perhaps going into buffers at the end of the sidings. The date and place is not known, although it is possibly somewhere in West London.
Credit STEAM: Harry Swindon Stratton 2

Fitters inspect Britannia class Pacific 70026 *Polar Star* as she is lifted back on the tracks. The locomotive was so badly damaged she had to be scrapped. On 20 November 1955 an accident occurred at Milton near Didcot. The inspector reported that: "the 8.30 a.m. excursion train from Treherbert to Paddington, became derailed at the facing crossover between the Main and the Goods lines. The derailment was caused by the excessive speed of the train through the sharply curved crossover." As the train tumbled down an embankment eleven passengers were killed and 157 injured, some seriously. **Credit STEAM A1/023**

Harrow and Wealdstone, 8 October 1952

The crash at Harrow and Wealdstone station happened at 8.19am on 8 October 1952. It is England's worst railway disaster and one of only three accidents in the United Kingdom in which more than one hundred people lost their lives. In total, 112 people died and more than 300 were injured. It was also a very rare triple collision where three trains collide with each other.

The morning of Wednesday 8 October turned out to be very foggy. The 7.31am Tring to Euston local passenger train stopped at Harrow and Wealdstone station, seven minutes late due to the fog. It had switched to the fast line just before the station to keep the slow lines to the south clear for empty stock movements. Carrying approximately 800 passengers, the train was much fuller than normal, as the previous service had been cancelled. At 8.19am, just as the guard was walking back to his brake van after checking doors on the last two carriages, the train was struck from behind by the night express from Perth travelling between 50 and 60mph.

The Perth sleeper train consisted of 46242 *City of Glasgow* with eleven carriages and some eighty-five passengers. Because of fog and other delays it was running approximately eighty minutes late.

A second or two after the first collision the 8am express from Euston to Liverpool and Manchester with its fifteen carriages and 200 passengers hauled by 45637 *Windward Islands* and 46202 *Princess Anne*, came through on the adjacent fast line in the opposite direction at about 60mph. The leading locomotive struck the *City of Glasgow* and came off the track. Sixteen carriages were destroyed, of which thirteen were concertinaed together under the station footbridge.

The HMRI report found that the sleeper train had passed a caution signal and two danger signals before colliding with the local train. Why this occurred will never be known as Driver Jones and Fireman Turnock, both experienced footplate crew, were killed in the crash. It is likely that the driver was concerned to make up time as the train was running very late and he and the firemen missed the warning signals in the fog.

The accident had two effects. Firstly it accelerated the introduction of the Automatic Warning System that told drivers that they had passed an adverse signal, although because of the cost, its arrival on many lines was very slow. And the crash confirmed the strength of the new all-steel carriages British Railways had begun to introduce as they were less severely damaged (and protected passengers better) than the older pre-war wood and steel carriages.

A subsequent Metropolitan Police report praised the response from the emergency services. Co-ordination on the spot was hampered, however, by the lack of communications equipment. There was only one walkie-talkie that, in the end, was not used. The only telephone was a walk away. An exotic element was the arrival of medical personnel from the neighbouring American base at Ruislip.

Because the accident happened on the outskirts of London there was huge media interest. As a result, unlike almost every other railway accident in this book, there is a large selection of photographs to choose from.

An aerial view showing the locomotives and carriages scattered along the platforms. The shot must have been taken fairly soon after the accident occurred as steam is still escaping from one of the engines. **Credit The National Archives RAIL 1007/638 (10)**

Rescuers pass a passenger on a stretcher over the wreckage. Some 300 passengers were injured some seriously in the accident. **Credit The National Archives RAIL 1007/638 (7)**

A female passenger is taken by stretcher along the track to a waiting ambulance. She must have been travelling on the Perth sleeper as wreckage of the *City of Glasgow* can be seen in the background. **Credit The National Archives RAIL 1007/638 (4)**

Two firemen help a passenger to safety. Judging by his dress he must have been in the Army. **Credit The National Archives RAIL 1007/638 (2)**

A number of local people rushed to help. Here women, including nuns from a local convent, are tearing up sheets to make bandages. **Credit The National Archives RAIL 1007/638 (3)**

Nearly 500 American medical personnel rushed to Harrow to help. Here a medical team provide blood to a passenger. One sergeant from Boston commented on the behaviour of the injured: 'The British don't cry'. **Credit: The National Archives RAIL 1007/638 (8)**

A fireman and an accident investigator inspect the wreckage of one of the carriages. **Credit The National Archives RAIL 1007/638 (6)**

APPENDIX 'A'

METROPOLITAN POLICE

"X" DIVISION   WEALDSTONE STATION

CASUALTIES RESULTING FROM LONDON MIDLAND REGION RAILWAY ACCIDENT AT HARROW AND WEALDSTONE STATION at 8.19 a.m. on WEDNESDAY, 8th OCTOBER, 1952

Key to Code : (F) Fatal.   (H.D.) Hospital detained.   (H.T.) Hospital treatment.

SERIAL No.	NAME	ADDRESS	CODE
1	ABBOTT, William	Seaford Green, Oxhey, Herts.	HD
2	ANDERSON, William	16, Richmond Drive, Watford	HT
3	ARMITAGE, Alfred	23, Strangeway, Watford	HT
4	ASHLEY, Ronald	16, Monifield Road, Broughty Ferry, Dundee	HD
5	AUSTIN, Robert John	4, Ladysmith Road, Wealdstone	F
6	BALDWIN, Kenneth	68, The Drive, West Harrow	HD
7	BANKS, Thomas	87, Western Road, Tring, Herts.	HT
8	BARBER, Stanley	38, Harris Road, Watford	HD
9	BARKER, Ronald	25, Seacroft Gardens, Oxhey, Herts.	HD
10	BARRATT, George	51, Southfield Avenue, Watford	HT
11	BATCHELOR, Frank	6, Oakdene Road, Watford	HT
12	BEARDER, Harold	35, Grange Avenue, Stanmore	HT
13	BEATTIE, John McCann	42, Powfoat Street, Glasgow	F
14	BEDWELL, Kenneth	119, Ashurst Road, Friern Barnet, Herts.	HD
15	BENJAFIELD, Ernest Albert	100, Winchester Road, Edmonton	F
16	BENNINGTON, Mr.	Mount Royal Hotel, W.1	HT
17	BENTIN, D.	30, Hill Street, Cheslyn Hay, Walsall, Staffs.	F
18	BENTLEY, Clifford Maurice	4, Alfred Street, Blockwick, Walsall, Staffs.	F
19	BINDLES, Mr.	Witts End, Pale Road, Watford	HT
20	BLAKE, H. G.	23, Hartford Avenue, Kenton	F
21	BLUNDELL, Horace	11, Woodcroft Avenue, Stanmore	F
22	BLUNDELL, Leonard	69, Grasmere Gardens, Harrow	F
23	BOWEN, Mrs.	94, Bushey Mill Crescent, Watford	HD
24	BRADDING, Mr.	75, Akeman Street, Tring, Herts.	HT
25	BREEZE, Beryl	81, Balmoral Road, Watford	HD
26	BRIERS, E. G.	7, Summerfield Road, Watford	F
27	BROOKS, H. N.	13, Corfe Close, Watford	F
28	BULPITT, Edgar William	33, Vernon Drive, Stanmore	HT
29	BURGESS, Walter Frederick	51, Dukes Avenue, Wealdstone	~~HT~~ F
30	BURT, James	16, Bulgear Drive, Paisley	HT
31	BURTENSHONE, Pauline	66, Bushey Mill Lane, Watford	HD
32	BURTON, Charles Harry	43, Sevington Road, Hendon	F
33	BURTON, Henry	88, Kensington Court, W.8	F
34	BURTON, Mrs. Polly	Pinconin, Michigan, U.S.A.	F
35	BUTTERWORTH, Eric	110, College Hill Road, Harrow Weald	HD
36	CARLILL, Edward	163a, High Street, Watford	HT
37	CASHMERE, Arthur	34, Watford Road, Kings Langley	HD
38	CHARLES, William	6, Bohn Grove, East Barnet	HD
39	CHEETHAM, Mrs. G.	50, Lower Morris Street, Wigan	F
40	CHICHLEY, Mrs.	154, Uppingham Avenue, Stanmore	HT
41	CHRISTOPHER, George Michael	131, Leggat Road, Watford	F
42	CHUBB, Mr. J. W.	39, Beaconsfield Road, Tring, Herts.	F
43	CLARK, C. G. F.	44, Furham, Feild, Hatch End	F
44	CLARK, George	31, Chester Road, Watford	F
45	CLARKE, Ethel	28, Weston Drive, Stanmore	HD
46	CLARKE, John	95, Eastcote Lane, South Harrow	HT

The Metropolitan Police produced a list of those who lost their lives in the crash. Many were commuters on their way to work in the City. Credit The National Archives MEPO 2/9291 (1)

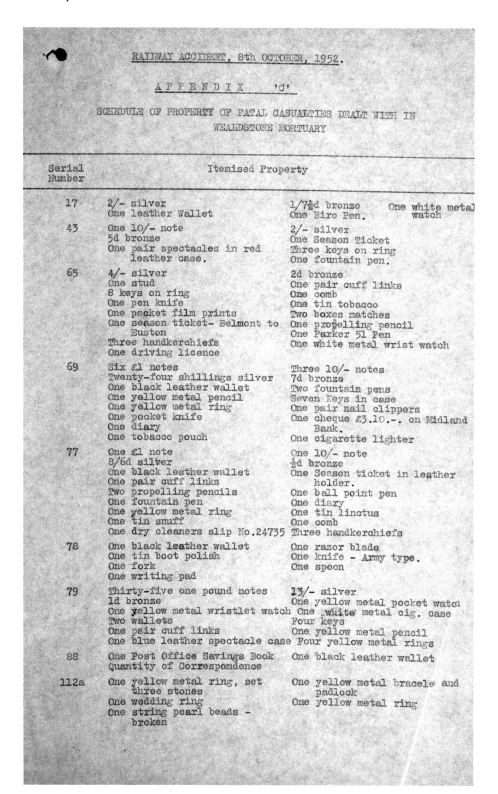

RAILWAY ACCIDENT, 8th OCTOBER, 1952.

APPENDIX 'C'

SCHEDULE OF PROPERTY OF FATAL CASUALTIES DEALT WITH IN
WEALDSTONE MORTUARY

Serial Number	Itemised Property	
17	2/- silver One leather Wallet	1/7½d bronze One white metal One Biro Pen. watch
43	One 10/- note 5d bronze One pair spectacles in red leather case.	2/- silver One Season Ticket Three keys on ring One fountain pen.
65	4/- silver One stud 8 keys on ring One pen knife One packet film prints One season ticket- Belmont to Euston Three handkerchiefs One driving licence	2d bronze One pair cuff links One comb One tin tobacco Two boxes matches One propelling pencil One Parker 51 Pen One white metal wrist watch
69	Six £1 notes Twenty-four shillings silver One black leather wallet One yellow metal pencil One yellow metal ring One pocket knife One diary One tobacco pouch	Three 10/- notes 7d bronze Two fountain pens Seven Keys in case One pair nail clippers One cheque £3.10.-. on Midland Bank. One cigarette lighter
77	One £1 note 8/6d silver One black leather wallet One pair cuff links Two propelling pencils One fountain pen One yellow metal ring One tin snuff One dry cleaners slip No.24735	One 10/- note ½d bronze One Season ticket in leather holder. One ball point pen One diary One tin linctus One comb Three handkerchiefs
78	One black leather wallet One tin boot polish One fork One writing pad	One razor blade One knife - Army type. One spoon
79	Thirty-five one pound notes 1d bronze One yellow metal wristlet watch Two wallets One pair cuff links One blue leather spectacle case	13/- silver One yellow metal pocket watch One white metal cig. case Four keys One yellow metal pencil Four yellow metal rings
88	One Post Office Savings Book Quantity of Correspondence	One black leather wallet

112a	One yellow metal ring, set
	    three stones
	One wedding ring
	One string pearl beads -
	    broken
		One yellow metal bracele and
		    padlock
		One yellow metal ring

The Metropolitan Police also itemised the lost property that was found on the three trains. Those items which were not reunited with their owners was sold or donated to the charitable fund set up to help the families of those who lost their lives in the crash. Credit The National Archives MEPO 2/9291 (2)

One of the priorities was to clear the mainline of debris so that services in and out of Euston could restart as soon as possible. Curious passengers stare out of the window at the clearance work going on. **Credit The National Archives RAIL 1007/638 (5)**

Further Reading

There are a number of excellent books on British railway accidents that are well worth looking out for. Although dated, the best book remains L.TC. Rolt, *Red for Danger* (2nd edition, Bodley Head, 1966 republished by The History Press, 2010). Almost as good is Nicholas Faith, *Derail: why trains crash* (Channel 4 Books, 2000). Others, which tend to be more technical in nature, include: J.A.B. Hamilton, *British Railway Accidents of the Twentieth Century* (Allen & Unwin, 1967), O.S. Nock, *Historic Railway Disasters* (Arrow, 1986) and Adrian Vaughan, *Danger Obstruction* (Ian Allen, 2008).

A number of the most important railway accidents are also described in *Fire and Stream* by Christian Wolmar (Atlantic, 2008): the best modern history of British railways. Also of interest is Matthew Engel's *Eleven Minutes Late: a train journey to the soul of Britain* (Macmillan, 2009). For railways of the nineteenth century look no further than Jack Simmons, *The Victorian Railway* (Thames & Hudson, 1991). A nice collection of articles about railways and railway history is Stuart Legge's *The Railway Book* (Fourth Estate, 1988).

There are also many books on particular railways and histories of various lines that describe railway accidents as appropriate. They tend to be written by enthusiasts for enthusiasts, concentrating on the technical rather than the human side of crashes.

There appear to be no websites specifically devoted to railway accidents and disasters, although Wikipedia describes all major British railway accidents often in some detail. An increasing number of accident reports and related documents can be found on the excellent Railway Archives website www.railwaysarchive.co.uk. If you are interested in finding more about signalling then the Signal Box should be able to help (www.signalbox.org). David Turner maintains an excellent blog on Victorian railways including a fascinating entry on railway accident insurance (http://turniprail.blogspot.co.uk).

Newspapers generally covered railway disasters in some detail. Many Victorian and Edwardian newspapers are now online in the British Newspaper Archive website www. britishnewspaperarchive.co.uk. Searching is free but you have to pay to download any stories.

For the ghoulish look out for this DVD in the Railways In Britain Archive series – *British Steam Railway Disasters 1913-1967* (2010). Clips about railway accidents can occasionally be found on YouTube, including Abermule (1921), Harrow and Wealdstone (1952) and Lewisham (1957).

In the introduction apart from the volumes listed above the following books were consulted: Charles F. Adams, *Railroad Accidents* (Putnam, 1879), *Mr Punch's Railway Book* (Educational Book Co, 1909), Wolfgang Schivelbusch, *The Railway Journey* (Blackwell, 1980), Jack Simmons (ed), *The Railway Traveller's Handy Book of Hints, Suggestions and Advice* (Adams and Dart, 1971) and Tom Standage, *The Victorian Internet* (Weidenfeld & Nicholson, 1998). In addition the quote about Charlie Peace came from A Life of Charlie Peace (www.bunker8.pwp.blueyonder. co.uk/history/Peace.htm), and current railway statistics were obtained from www.rail-reg.gov.uk and www.dft.gov.uk/statistics/releases/reported-road-casualties-gb-main-results-2011.